the poet confronts bukowski's ghost

kat giordano

Copyright © 2018 by Kat Giordano.
All rights reserved.

Published by Philosophical Idiot
Phillipsburg, NJ
www.philosophicalidiot.com

Cover by James Swanick.

No part of this book may be reproduced or transmitted
in any form without written consent from
the author/publisher, except where permitted by law.

Every person in this book is "imaginary."
Any resemblance to actual people, living or dead,
is "purely coincidental." This book
is presented as a work of "fictional" "poetry."

Previous drafts of these poems have been featured by
Up the Staircase Quarterly, *Rat's Ass Review*, *The Cincinnati Review*
Indigent Press, *CLASH Media*, *OCCULUM*, *Ucity Review*,
the *Online Review of Books and Current Affairs*,
Maudlin House, *Winedrunk Sidewalk*, and *Philosophical Idiot*.

IBSN-13: 9781732292208
ISBN-10: 1723392205

For B., my best friend, soulmate, vital organ, etc. etc.

Thanks for everything you'll spend the rest of your life telling me was "nothing, really."

I love you in a way I didn't think people loved each other in real life (and now it's in my very first book forever, so we'd better not fuck this up).

"Of course it's possible to love a human being
if you don't know them too well."

Charles Bukowski, *Notes of a Dirty Old Man*

once something is dirty, i can get as many stains on it as i want.

STYLE	17
TWO BUCKETS	19
NEW YEAR'S DAY	20
GARBAGE	21
HOUSE HUNTING	22
THE MOMENT THAT TRUTH IS ORGANIZED IT BECOMES A LIE	25
THE WAFER ON OUR TONGUES	26
ONCE YOU GO IN YOU ALWAYS COME OUT ALIVE	27
FOR GOOD	28
RELATABLE MEMES	29
I WOULD NEVER EAT AVOCADO TOAST AGAIN IF WE COULD LIVE IN A HOUSE TOGETHER & SMOKE WEED ON THE ROOF	30
ARS POETICA I	32
A ONE-NIGHT STAND	34
I ONLY SKATE WHEN I HAVE EMOTIONAL TRAUMA	36
LIVING WITH ANXIETY	37
I SAW OWEN WILSON ONE TIME FROM A DISTANCE AND WE JUST STARED AT EACH OTHER, THEN HIS CAR DROVE OFF	39

it's just pessimism making us lucky.

A CONFESSION	43
THE FIGHT	45
ME & THE OX	46
I KNOW YOU COULD TAKE ME IF YOU WANTED TO, SO I CHOOSE TO ERR ON THE SIDE OF CAUTION	48
RECONCILIATION	49
POET MAN	50
EITHER I LIE TO YOU OR WE CRY TOGETHER	53
BOB ROSS & YOU	54
HYPOTHESIS IN A DIVE BAR, 1:18 A.M.	55
I BLUSH WHEN YOU SAY I HAVE A GHOSTWRITER	56
HOW TO BURN ASHES	57
MYSTERY FLAVOR	58
MEDITATION ON LONELINESS WHILE TEARFULLY BINGE-EATING HONEY NUT CHEERIOS IN MY UNDERWEAR AT 3:47 A.M.	59
THE EIGHTH DAY	60

*throwing yourself on that serrated edge
will not love it into softness.*

SAVED	63
WATER IN THE EYES AND ALCOHOL IN THE EYES ARE PRETTY MUCH THE SAME I KNOW THIS FROM FIRST HAND EXPERIENCE	65
SAY WHEN	66
I'M AFRAID	67
ON CONFIDENCE	68
THE POET CONFRONTS BUKOWSKI'S GHOST	70
VOICE TO TEXT	74
NARRATIVE	75
ARS POETICA II	76
TO THE MAN WHO SAID READING MY POETRY WAS "MORE INTIMATE THAN SEX"	78
YOU SAW YOURSELF IN ME & WANTED TO DIE	79
THE WORST MISSED CONNECTION OF MY LIFE	80
YOU LET A SNAKE LOOSE IN MY HOUSE	81
NOTHING BUT OLD LINT	82
YOU WILL BE SEEING UNUSUAL ACCOMPLISHMENT	83

LETTER FOR A FAN	84
I JUST WANTED YOU TO KNOW THAT SOMEONE LOVES YOU BAD	85
THE TRUEST POEM I WROTE ABOUT YOU	86
A POEM IS BULLSHIT AT THE BOTTOM OF THE OCEAN	88
I NEARLY HAD A PANIC ATTACK WHILE RUSHING TO GET LUNCH BECAUSE A MAN ON THE STREET WHO LOOKED LIKE A GOBLIN STARTED SPEAKING IN TONGUES AT ME & I'D HAD SO MUCH COFFEE & HE WAS SO GOBLIN-LIKE THAT I BRIEFLY CONSIDERED THE POSSIBILITY THAT GOBLINS WERE REAL & HE WAS A REAL GOBLIN	89
WHY BEES STING (EVEN KNOWING WHAT WILL HAPPEN)	90

i see all of the too much, too.

FOLK SONG	93
BEST BEFORE	96
LOVE DOESN'T EXIST, CHANGE MY VIEW	97
INTIMATE BIOGRAPHY OF A NARCISSIST	98
THE POMEGRANATE ONE	99
REAL WISDOM	101
IT'S FINE	102
POEM AFTER REALIZING YOUR ENTIRE FAMILY UNFRIENDED ME ON FACEBOOK	104
NO IT'S COOL, NEVERMIND, I WAS PROBABLY JUST BEING DRAMATIC	105
CONSPIRACY THEORY	106
I LOVE YOU	107
POETRY IS NOT SELF-EXPRESSION	108
PACKING THE WOUND	109
TO YOU, AFTER YOU'VE READ MY POEMS	111

once something is dirty, i can get as many stains on it as i want.

STYLE

it's true what Bukowski said about style –
it really is the answer to everything:

it's late. we cross paths in front of a 7-11
at which point I lunge forward, swiping
your wallet right out of your shorts.
you're stunned. you say *what the hell?*
and I simply stammer, paralyzed
by my own shock at what I've just done.
there is no getaway. the cops are called,
and that's how you remember me.

now, the same scenario: near-midnight,
the 7-11 on Smithfield, me and you,
only this time, a hug instead of a lunge,
so that my one hand is poaching your wallet
and the other remains innocent, gently rubbing
your back as I try to place the musk of your collar
out of my mind. I whisper *have a wonderful night*
and then disappear into a cloud of smoke
and it's only five minutes later at the register
that you realize your wallet is missing. I vanish
without having to answer for it, forever
a mirage in your memory, a fleeting moment
where you ached something awful in your jeans.

mess is inevitable. the real moral duty
lies in making the right one: a fucked-up thing so loud
it can't be contained in a grimace.

Hemingway blew his brains out.
I'm into that. hell, anybody who leaves
behind a note should earn some points.
life may be precious and short and singular
but style is holy, a smoke bomb in my coat
to be set off only when the time is right,
something symbolic, or maybe televised.

that way, it'll count.

TWO BUCKETS

It's hard to tell if I'm the aching or the ache
sometimes. I don't always know
if I'm the guy or the empty fridge
he keeps opening, trying to materialize a snack.

I once found a chicken foot in a chicken finger
and tweeted a photo to the company.
Their response was a coupon for more chicken

like I'd still want it after that.
I once had a poet I admired tell me I would never be great
without him, just some girl with a boyfriend.
I told him off and then won a prize

for a poem I wrote about it. I once did some drugs
to forget about the drugs I'd already done, like how you might
take another lover, hope they shake you with enough force
to dislodge the old one from your bones
like a gut punch to a popcorn kernel, and by that I mean
even if you could breathe again,
there'd be a brand-new bruise to deal with. I am

also the bruise. The doctor. The patient. The arm
he holds up every minute to see if it still hurts.

I have lost track of the narrative,
the past and present just two buckets
dumping into each other at once. An attached
pair of hands I won't look at
for fear I might see something I recognize,
or don't.

NEW YEAR'S DAY

i haven't cried at all this year
and please don't tell me what day
it is. i don't know how long
it will last, only that today
is not the usual unmade bed
i wake up cried-out and sore in,
that what you need must be
begged from some brink or another
into existence, a punchline
at the end of pain, like
being waterboarded by your own life.

i don't know what i'm saying except
i'm in love with everyone and afraid
of the weight of it, how when my body
vibrates at this frequency it so easily
turns me on. what would it mean
not to wait this time for what's
after sadness, to steal the map
and fold those coasts closer
together like my own god?

i think i should just go to bed
more often. i think i should rip open,
turn the camera on the animal
i am. i think i should plunge myself
face-first into the tub now, stop counting,
let my lungs engorge as they will.

GARBAGE

lately i call so many things garbage
that when i went to go take out my trash
last week, i couldn't find the word.
i hate how much irony it takes
to keep the motor running, the lights on
in the useless room behind my eyes
where one mirror pouts into another,
quoting lines from a movie
written by somebody else.

sometimes i wish comparing a lover to
a summer's day were still up for grabs,
that i could look at a sunset and
honest-to-god actually buy it.
i want to turn to you and sigh something
that doesn't come out of a can,
like, *when you swipe your fingers*
between my thighs like that
it's like someone smashing
the motherfucking like button
on all of my tweets at once,
so hideous and hot it burns down
every Wal-Mart® on the planet.

but then where would you go
when you wanted to find me?

HOUSE HUNTING

Why is it that nobody in any fucking HGTV show
remembers they can repaint their fucking house?
They're blind, all of these white-bread families, laughing
as they walk together from property to gorgeous property
in some unattainable corner of California,
or some swanky island out in the middle of nowhere
where every house overlooks the water but they still need
a fucking swimming pool for some reason. They only see
what's missing, the mistakes, the outdated cabinets,
the damaged floors, and the wall color that isn't quite
Their Style. *Fuck your style*, I want to say, *and fuck
that you can afford to be so particular about something
this easy to change.* Not everything is ready right away.
Kitchens can be remodeled. *Put down an area rug for now,*
I want to say, *and repaint your fucking living room.*

And is it me, or does every couple on that channel have
issues way beyond the scope of home improvement?
Their poorly-hidden resentment bubbles
below every conversation they have
on camera. They may be talking about the location
of House #2 or discussing the budget for their first
flip, but if you listen closely you can hear them getting
tetchy and you might notice the show going to commercial
just before one of them snaps. The editing encourages you
to play it off as casual disagreement, but as a discerning viewer
I have to ask myself what the fuck's wrong with these people
and why they waited to discuss the wish list for their future
home until whenever they were being filmed for a TV show.

What I mean to say is it's bad when you love someone
so much you're unable to watch even bland, inoffensive TV.
I've found few things in life universally satisfying
but TV was one of them. I was never really entertained
but it used to shut me off for a while, no matter how
I felt. Now all I feel is anger. As I watch, I sink
into the couch. The scowl of utter disgust
never leaves my face. The word "square-footage"
sends me into such a tizzy I could rip an infant in half.
Sometimes I tune out the show entirely and my eyes
follow the couples around the screen while I imagine
wallpapering their dumb fucking mouths shut. I become
so warped by rage I can hardly recognize myself; I feel
it happening but still all I can think about is how you and I
are so much better than all of these stupid people.

We would do everything right. They wouldn't be able to
fill an episode with us because when we'd call up the
real estate agent, we'd already know exactly where
we wanted to live. There would be no arguments
for the producers to editorialize, no outlandish requests.
Give us the ugly fucking cabinets. The stains on the floor
don't bother us. We're smart enough to know that
the piss-yellow walls are what's holding this place
together, and even if they aren't we can paint them
ourselves. We'd be okay with a fixer-upper because we know
that sometimes something amazing takes a long time.

But you're miles away from me, and we only have receipts
and crumpled singles in our wallets. Sometimes
you visit me and we drive around, pointing out
all of the little blue houses we see, and that's the closest
we ever get to house-hunting. I hope someday
I'll be able to sit around with you on a Tuesday night
and we can put on this dumb fucking channel
and you can say that thing you always say about how
the best things on HGTV are the commercials. Then
I'll sit through an entire episode without getting
angry at all of the couples who don't deserve
these houses, these cameras, these lives. There will only be
the quiet glow of superiority that comes
from knowing they'll never know what it's like
to wait this long and then kick this much ass.

THE MOMENT THAT TRUTH IS ORGANIZED IT BECOMES A LIE

1. I'm worried this isn't even a poem.

2. Fuck it.

3. Writing a poem like this feels a lot like taking one of those online personality quizzes. Whenever I lock in an answer I can't help but predict exactly what the quiz means by its question, leading me to pick the answers that represent the result I want, rather than the Right Answers, which in turn defeats the entire purpose of taking the quiz in the first place.

4. Or maybe those results are the Right ones in that they show me the fruit of my narcissism, what happens when I try to trick the mirror into showing me a more flattering reflection.

5. In other words, you can never be honest in a poem. I'm telling you that now, so believe me.

6. I'm walking you through a gallery of all of my favorite images of me. There's not one photo here I'm blinking in. This is only what I look like when I know someone is looking.

THE WAFER ON OUR TONGUES

Maybe it's just another one of the lies
they feed us, the notion that anything can happen
at all, and we all settle because we want anything
to be true. Now that we know the truth
about the Easter Bunny, about the drugs
that couldn't save us and only made us feel
good. Now that we're all out of rocket ships.
Now that we have nothing but lint in our pockets.
One day I'll have to hold my kid in my arms,
guide his chin to the sky and admit
we thought there'd be flying cars by now.
I'll pull a TV out of my pocket and show him
the old cartoons from the '90s when we still fought
over the remote, thought it was any better than going
to church. I'll tell him about when we were forced to go,
the wafer they placed on our tongues, the taste
of half-digested bread. How we did it to ensure
we had somewhere safe to go when everything
crumbled. I'll tell him there used to be a word
for a place like that, and I'll suck my teeth awhile,
trying to remember it, retracing my steps for it,
like some old toy I must have misplaced.

ONCE YOU GO IN YOU ALWAYS COME OUT ALIVE

The piano falls on your head and you become some crinkled accordion, swaying for a few seconds but always popping back into shape. Laugh track. Credits. The black that comes after. That's the part that gets me. You watch the show but don't stay long enough to see the silence wash jaggedly over the room like a memory of a memory. But I listen, maybe too much. I follow your instructions. Close eyes. Picture beach. Smell ocean. I'm supposed to be okay then, staring out. But isn't it all just something we do while we're waiting? Isn't it all just an hourglass basin trickling down? I'm sitting in a room that you tell me we're sitting in together but I'm the only one who smells it burning. I, a piece of kindling cut from some other piece of kindling. I, some will-less domino in a string of will-less dominos. I, a freak-accident of purposeless cells trying to become more than themselves. We can drink and fuck all we want but we're only ever filling holes. You hold me and I don't know how to tell you we aren't really touching each other. Do you think we'll wake up after all of this is over? Will it even be worth it to come back?

FOR GOOD

The anger came suddenly. I was
a child who started failing the fourth grade
and only then realized with a jolt
that I never had a choice in attending.
I realized my first breath had trickled
through me on its own. The rest was
my problem. I stayed up for weeks, imagining
my aging body a Mylar birthday balloon
with nothing left to do but die. The anger

was worse than the days I wished it would happen:
a sudden blackness, absolving. I was at the end
of a movie where the main character wakes up
only to find the whole adventure was a dream.
Tricked. I saw young children doomed
already in the spring of their lives, and I pouted.
I took a class on climate change and our ending world
but I didn't go, didn't have to. My boyfriend left
on a beer run and I flung his body through
a thousand bloody accidents. To this day

I taste the suffering in every chicken wing
I eat. I collapse when I pass crashed cars
and roadkill, nostalgic for the days
I'd insert myself into such a scene,
roasting for good on the bloody asphalt,
guts splayed out among crushed cartons
and debris, not having yet remembered
the thing I forgot I'd forgotten.

RELATABLE MEMES

when you wake up every morning
in a glue trap that you laid yourself.

when the waitress asks you what you want
and you say, *i want the days to stop*
hiding behind these increasingly heavier curtains.
i want those i've deemed responsible
for protecting my heart to feel
guilty for sleeping on the job. i want everyone
i love to bloom but not this much
quicker than me, not all at once, not
if I end up by myself,
and nobody laughs
because nobody but you
is in on the joke.

I WOULD NEVER EAT AVOCADO TOAST AGAIN IF WE COULD LIVE IN A HOUSE TOGETHER & SMOKE WEED ON THE ROOF

We'd get a really nice Persian rug to spread over the floor and it'd be the only nice thing we'd own.

Every time we'd have a party our friends would have to sit on it and we'd hover over them the whole night, making sure they used napkins with their chips and salsa to catch the drippings.

If somebody passed out on it we'd gently lift their head up and slide a washcloth underneath to catch any spit-up. The best parts would be the mornings when everyone'd stumble out of the place hungover and leave us by ourselves. We'd sigh with relief every time, knowing we'd protected our rug yet again, both of us secretly wishing we hadn't.

When I was 12 my parents got a new couch for the attic and it was bright white and terrifying. The first thing I ever spilled on it was Diet Barq's Root Beer. I knocked it out of my crush's hand while trying to prevent him from seeing my selfies on the 2 megapixel Nikon my grandpop got me for Christmas. Later I took a photo with my eyes crossed and followed a Photoshop tutorial to surround myself in realistic-looking pink bubbles.

It got a lot of likes on Facebook.

I used to only post pictures of myself with straightened hair but I got over it after my aunt tagged me in a photo from Halloween where my hair was wet and I was dressed like Popeye the Sailor. Once something is dirty, I can get as many stains on it as I want.

I used to call you every night but now I just send a Bitmoji of myself with a cat on my head.

I used to try and leave my bed by noon but now sometimes I don't leave it at all.

I used to only let myself eat perishables in my room but last week I had Mini Wheats and left the bowl of milk on my dresser for days until it grew a culture.

It's the beginning of summer, one of the first yellow, sticky afternoons, and from my spot on my paisley-pink childhood sheets I can hear the neighborhood kids fighting with each other.

I'm lying in bed at 4 PM with my hair still wrapped in a towel, completing a Facebook quiz called "What will your friends do when you go missing?" I grant it permission to access my wall and friends list, but it doesn't load the page.

ARS POETICA I

If a man held a gun to my head
and forced me to lose either you
or a chunk of my temporal lobe, I'd purge
the shape of you from my mouth's memory
and walk away whole with my skull
intact, gaslight all my friends by pretending
I never dreamed of affixing you to me
in front of God and everyone.

We can't measure up to the love
that came before us: those old dudes
chasing passion through the desert
in cars driven by total strangers, subsisting
on whiskey and frantic sex with hands
weathered by pub smoke and highway sun,
all on the off-chance that they'd find you
in the next town over, or that the next guy
whose couch they'd crash on would have
directions to your place.

I'd never do those things for you.
I like my shaved legs, my hot showers,
my own bed, and I don't ride
with strangers unless an app tells me to
and it costs me seven dollars.
You roll up to my house but I'm busy
with my Sims family. I blow you off
to make computer people fuck their neighbors
behind their partners' backs and then
piss all over the floor.

And what about those nights I get set up
with a whiskey and a Big Mood
but your phone's off until the morning?
And those parties where I tell my friends
they'll finally get to meet you
and you don't show up
'til the end of the night, half-dressed,
strung out, and cursing to yourself
and won't look them in the eye?

We both deserve better. I fantasize sometimes
about changing my number and just taking off
but I'm weak, and it's too fucking good
when it's good in the dark with you
at 2 AM when we're still a little high,
and my sheets are still folded up on the edge
of the bed, and you say those things
into my mouth, and I'm somebody
who has somebody, or something close.

A ONE-NIGHT STAND

The kind where you don't touch
but wake up in the same sort of haze,
feeling spent. That same wanting-more,
though just yesterday you didn't
know how much there was to want.
Intimacy leaves a predictable stain,
marking the carelessness
that happens when two decide
honesty, at any cost,
can no longer be contained.

It was a mess only we could make,
a dull headache only Captain and Coke
could leave behind. The unmistakeable
timbre of the words *beautiful*
and *love* after years of restraint
within my stomach. Your straining
cry. My hands in your hair
like a baby. I held you, and the night
unfolded around us, spill after
spill, each one more irreversible
than the last.

It all risks melodrama:
waking up from this kind of wild
confession, swaddling
a shaking friend into coherence,
and thinking in the back of the cab home
that what you have seen is more
sacred than a naked body.

It's what makes nights like this
into what they are:
a frantic scramble for the parts we have
always longed to touch, the beginning
of a lifetime spent scheming our way
back for the rest.

I ONLY SKATE WHEN I HAVE EMOTIONAL TRAUMA

it's got to be evening. i wait 'til the street lights click on and i go out to the creek behind the middle school to grind the length of the old bridge in the dark. i tell no one. i leave my phone at home and flip my hood down over my eyes and i feel like a monk with holy purpose, unattached, in need of nothing. no fish-eye. no friends. only the screech of my trucks on old metal, that old handrail groaning. it's better that way.

LIVING WITH ANXIETY

He's convinced that something horrible is always lurking
in the dark. So when I come home, all of the lamps
are on, the exhaust whirring, huffing nonexistent
licks of smoke. I find him checking the oven for
burnt edges on the cookies he put in two minutes ago.
With a trembling finger he flicks the oven light on and off,
his un-mitted hand fondling his neck for new tumors
the past ten inspections may have missed. The chocolate
chips, he later explains, make his lips tingle, activate
his decades-latent allergy. I finish the others
by his side while his timer ticks down. "Anaphylactic shock
occurs within thirty minutes of ingestion," he explains.

It doesn't.

Everything he owns is kept in plain sight, piled
either on his desk or the floor.
He needs everything at his fingertips
for whenever the big disaster finally happens. Once,
the smoke alarm in our building went off during the night
and he slept in his shoes for the next month.

My friends say he's harmless and even pity him for being
afraid to live, afraid of someone he loves dying,
or getting hurt, or needing something he has already
thrown out. But I don't think he's afraid. I think
he wants it to happen, craves the relief of a good tragedy,
like a test he's been studying for his whole life.

I once walked in on him touching himself
to a disaster movie. A man had just watched
his best friend jump out of a collapsing building
and splatter on the ground five stories below.
Seeing this, the man crouched down and wept
in the flames. I heard my anxiety sigh,
his white limbs tensing, then going limp.
It was the calmest I'd ever seen him,
and I've gotta tell you, I'd never been more afraid.

I SAW OWEN WILSON ONE TIME FROM A DISTANCE AND WE JUST STARED AT EACH OTHER, THEN HIS CAR DROVE OFF

In the story I tell myself, things are different. He pulls a rather dangerous U-ey at the next intersection and parallel-parks on the other side of the street. I cross over like my legs are being controlled by someone else and I almost get hit by a car before I make it to the other curb, but I do make it there – just as he's getting out of his Porsche. He smiles. I don't say my first thought, which is that someone with a Porsche shouldn't drive like an asshole. You'd think a man who starred in not one, not two, but three animated movies about sentient automobiles would know that. Anyway, he's there, and I'm there, and we give each other this look. *Hey you*, he says. *Hey Lightning McQueen*, I say. His resulting shoulder-punch sends thousands of volts through both of our bodies. He asks if I wanna get out of here and I say yes, even though I was actually on my way to meet you.

Cut to a scene inside of his car in some deserted parking lot where Delilah is playing on the radio and we're sighing into each other's mouths to drown out her voice – me, a jammed-up printer; him, a Dyson vacuum. Our legs wind around each other; our hands are in each other's hair – his, a field of wheat; mine, a clump of brambles. I glide my lips down his stomach and peer up at him from the fly of his pants and I know he won't say anything weird about my nose because his is identical and he says, *hey you*, and I say, *hey Lightning McQueen*. I fiddle with the brass knob of his jeans but then his phone goes off. He lets it vibrate in his pocket against my forearm a few times and then answers, and mostly nods a lot, and then hangs up. *Pixar*, I say, knowing somehow. *Pixar*, he says. *They're thinking about* Cars 4, he says, *and they want to meet with me now*. I say I understand and he drives me home but by then it's too late to call you, so I just sigh myself to sleep.

The next day, I tell you all of this and you understand and everything is forgiven because, I mean, it's Owen Wilson. But the truth is, I was never on my way to you. The truth is, I never even saw Owen Wilson. The truth is, I was too scared to get out of bed. And even if I had, if I had been walking down the road and he'd driven past me, I would have been too busy counting steps in my head to look up.

it's just pessimism making us lucky.

A CONFESSION

There was this one guy in high school my friend
and I used to laugh about, the kind
who has something off about them
but not anything pathological or diagnosable,
so it felt okay at the time that he became

kind of a meme to us. His online presence
was the main object of our ridicule, his
Facebook feed boasting every goddamn detail
of his life. We watched the rise and fall
of a dozen different relationships with dark-haired girls

with just first and middle names who were also
a mess. My friend or I would begin online chats
in hysterics, and the other would check, validate

the cringe-inducing spectacle that was his life:
an amalgam of multi-paragraph confessions
of love, rants about billiards, walkthroughs he made
for whatever first-person shooter was popular

at the time. I wasn't ashamed enough
when one day, he called me out for liking too many
of his posts in a row, which I did often and didn't mean
one-hundred-percent ironically, because
I did like them, in my own snarky way. Instead
I scoffed at his bold accusation, took a screenshot,
and sent it to my friend so we could

laugh. We don't do that so much anymore
but I can't delete him. I'm still interested
in his daily life as a Sears sales guy, his
nebulous attempt at professional wrestling
for a living. I absorb every detail of his dumb life
and graft it, pathetically, to my own.

Leaving work today, I logged in and saw his latest
update: he slept 18 hours, had some complex dream
about one of the many dark-haired women
of his past. Gently, he reassures the audience
that later today he'll post a video summarizing
each gut-wrenching moment. I convince myself
I won't watch, but my phone burns a hole
in my pocket as I'm walking home.

THE FIGHT

the fight
is not always a fist
or a bleeding mouth,
a pain you can put ice on.

what if the bell rings for me
in a diner? i can't Put 'Em Up
with chicken fingers in my hands.
the elbow room for a right hook
just isn't there. the friend i'm with
wouldn't want to watch me
make a fucker bleed,
so i breathe, fumbling for jokes
while my demons swat my legs from the floor.

the sweaty pay-per-view fantasy
is great for some, but my fight
is for the diners i haven't gone to,
and i can't read the menu
with a steak on my eye.

ME & THE OX

We never touched, but we stared
at each other once through a fog
of pizza-coma and pot smoke
and I saw his tiny button-eyes piercing the gulf
between his and mine. The gaze was nothing
like desire, but instead an invitation
to tame, my awe like a lotus blooming
somewhere deep down, untouchable
and unseen. He breathed and I focused
on his breath, shivering as it passed through
his flaring nostrils like drapes billowing,
the first indication that a porthole to
something cold and unknown had opened.

A shiver, and then a split-second spiral
into doubt: how would I explain him
to my roommate? Another ornery beast
I'd dragged home without asking, another phase
who'll leave behind structural damage, a mess
I'll be no good at cleaning up. My friends
would never come near me again for fear
they'd misspeak and I'd sic him on them
like some kind of protector trained to defend
my delusion. I could tame him, but then I'd be
all alone. For a moment I mourned
what could have been: me ambling on his back
through an untouched meadow, the wind
brushing his fur back toward my clinging hands.

And on any other day, I would tell you
that I still dream of him sometimes, the way some
will pine for decades over the same lost love,
lying awake at night in agony over what I could
do or say to once again see him leering at me
through the fog. But I'm not like those forlorn
ex-lovers who tirelessly audit the past. The ox and I
were no good together. In real life,
he is a beast and I am a tiny China shop quivering
in the wind. If we'd touched, we'd have hurt
each other – my face shattered with hoofprints,
his lips blue from the lead I'd force around his neck.

I KNOW YOU COULD TAKE ME IF YOU WANTED TO, SO I CHOOSE TO ERR ON THE SIDE OF CAUTION

i blow up your photo and use it like a poison bandaid,
pasting it wherever i want the pain to last:
the vegetable crisper, the alarm clock, the base of the jar
where i store my weed. i trim you down for the soles of my heels
so i can blame you for each agonizing step.

RECONCILIATION

I have never once purposely hurt or endangered
another person, never once sat in my room planning
the suffering of enemies, let alone friends.
Yet nightly, I lament
my many transgressions: not nodding
at the waiter who says *enjoy*,
letting the door slam shut on the girl
carrying that heavy package,
the way I look at you when you tell me
I don't need to *make* you love me. I offer

my shame up to the void, paying special attention
to each breach of courtesy that may have stained me,
even briefly, as someone hardly worth forgiving,
loving. I spend my nights groveling at the feet of false idols
molded to resemble the people I love, shuddering
each time the light glints off their eyes. I imagine

the day you give up, it will be for some other
reason, like your feelings filtering quietly
between your fingers like so much sand, imperceptible.
But they still haunt me, my many trespasses,
and creep towards me from the corners of my room.

POET MAN

Poet Man likes to write about taking random women home from the bar on a Wednesday night. Not women like you, though. Capital-W Women, the willowy kind who don't talk. The whole world is full of talking and Poet Man wants someone to listen to him and touch him and not need anything at all. He does them on the frameless mattress in the corner of his rented room and talks death at them in the few minutes between cumming and falling asleep. The Women leave the next morning and in his poems Poet Man wonders why the world is so impersonal. All of these people talking but none of them hearing each other. People never listen to each other these days, says Poet Man. You agree for a second but Poet Man has already begun masturbating to the emptiness he feels when caressing random bodies. Or something. Poet Man smokes a cigarette. Poet Man drinks a whiskey. Poet Man falls asleep with his dick in his hand.

You catch Poet Man after the reading and you tell Poet Man you thought his work was brilliant. You say it illustrates perfectly the struggles of mental illness and isolation. Poet Man smiles like you would at a baby in the grocery store before informing you that mental disorders are a myth and that the poem was really getting at the universal hopelessness of the contemporary American male – a sure-fire way, he says, to shake up the poetry world. You nod uneasily and Poet Man takes your hand without asking. Poet Man tells you you're actually very smart and invites you out for drinks. It's 4:00, you say. Time is a construct, says Poet Man.

Poet Man insists on the most expensive bar in the neighborhood and doesn't offer to pay because Poet Man thinks gender roles are archaic and identity politics are holding us back. You nod quietly for the rest of the night and as you're signing off on the bill for your $15 order of two beers Poet Man thanks you. You ask Poet Man what for and Poet Man says for not being cruel because most women are so cruel, so heartless. They only lead to pain. It's so tragic, he says, to want to touch a woman. So tragic, so tragic, so tragic. When you get to his place he repeats the phrase over and over again from on top of you while you wonder why there isn't any soap in his bathroom. Poet Man smokes a cigarette.

You pull your clothes back on and Poet Man asks you if you've ever thought of killing yourself. You tell him the story of when you were a freshman in college and learned about depression and got on medication. Poet Man says he doesn't believe in depression, because how can you live in a world like this and not want so badly to die? Because intelligence, says Poet Man, is a burden. You tell Poet Man you don't feel burdened anymore since getting on the meds and Poet Man says exactly, and depending on all of these chemicals is killing you. Then Poet Man smokes another cigarette.

You get up to leave and when you offer to give Poet Man your number he shakes his head sagely and says he doesn't believe in second encounters because after all what are we but hopeless specs in a lonely universe destined to be alone so why bother? So you leave.

A few months later, you're reading from your chapbook and spot Poet Man in the audience. You two share a grin so you catch up after it's over. I see you cut your hair short, says Poet Man. You nod. What is it with you and the nodding? I prefer long-haired women myself, says Poet Man. You tell Poet Man you were getting sick of styling your long hair in the morning and Poet Man warns you not to care so much about how you look. It's shallow, he says, so shallow and tragic and anyway what have you been up to? You shrug and say you just moved in with your new girlfriend who you met at a protest. Good, says Poet Man. I always thought you would be better with a woman. Someone like you would be too cruel to a man. You tell Poet Man you're actually bisexual and Poet Man says, oh, again with the identity politics. Anyway, those poems were actually great. Actually? you ask, and Poet Man smiles to himself and explains they just weren't what he'd expected and he liked the one about the Poet Man. It's so universal, he says, taking a long drag of his cigarette.

EITHER I LIE TO YOU
OR WE CRY TOGETHER

For a moment back there I thought about emptying like an overstuffed garbage bag, bursting and leaking onto the pristine linoleum, leaving you to fish through everything everybody else discarded. You were good at finding me when the rest of them said you wouldn't, when I was hiding in the under-sink cabinet in the dark, empty and balled-up beneath the leaky garbage disposal and all of the junk. You laid me in kitchen-window sunbeams and looked at me like only somebody without nostrils could look at me, like I could be good. You made plans to protect me from flies in the garden when I was too heavy to drag out of bed.

So I wanted your gloved hands rooting through the crime scene of my body. I wanted the hum of your Kenmore fridge to be the last sound I ever heard. I wanted to fall apart dangling from your wrist, to squint into your fading face as you plucked the flies from me like a saint. I knew you could clean up the mess, even though it wasn't yours. I knew deep down you would be good to me, even when I'd never been good. I realized that you could take it.

Put me outside while you can. Lay me against the two steel cans out on the curb. Sleep in while the trucks come; be too busy dreaming of someone else to be disturbed by their groan. Do what you could never do with me. Walk in the garden. Read a book in our bed by the lamplight without holding your nose. Put me out now while it still counts, while the house is still spotless, while there is still time to become accustomed to something other than dirt. It'll hurt now, but I promise it'll be worth it.

BOB ROSS & YOU

After so many evergreens scratched into mountains,
you might be curious, might want to see him wail onto canvas
some shameful vestige of his Air Force days –
loud enough to shake the joint from your fingers,
transport you to some dingy bathroom where he's
hounding you to clean the latrine. But he won't do it,
insisting instead on some lesser sharpness,
twin peaks blending into a clutter of happy little trees.
You take a toke, deflating, watch him just beat the devil
out of that two-inch brush. A stream bubbles to life,
the current hurtling it out towards the mist.
A little detail, he coos, *is just enough*. No need for
the assaulting sharpness of the flowering brush.
He leaves the foreground unobscured, as if inviting you
to round the riverbend with him and feel as if,
for a moment, it can be that way forever.

HYPOTHESIS IN A DIVE BAR, 1:18 A.M.

Even from here, I can picture the potential tangle
of our legs — ritual, no real meaning,
the same way headphone wires find each other inside
of a jacket pocket. Unsentimental. Just

the way things are. A health class textbook diagram
we're just desperate enough to jack off to. You would
kneel down at my feet like a one-man congregation,
taking every stiff moan as your sermon, and I'd keep preaching
as long as it kept resembling truth. Not because I like to
lie, but because when you'd look up at me like someone
who knew the answer, I'd want so badly to have one. And you

would have one, eventually, the way trying every single frequency
in your car stereo means you'll eventually hear something
like music. It'll make sense to you that it just happens
to be "The Boys Are Back in Town" on repeat because for you,
at that moment, all your boys are finally coming back into town.
But I don't want to spend the rest of my life being played
over and over again in a diner off the turnpike, making
all the worn-down waitresses roll their eyes while we try
to mimic something we saw once in a film our parents
didn't want us to see. So I'll pretend I don't notice

you staring like you're stoned and I'm a Tombstone pizza,
but I'll still hoard your dumb open mouth like the pack
of open oyster crackers inside my glove box:
nothing like the real thing, but it'll help in a pinch
if you're desperate or have enough of an imagination
to forget exactly where it came from.

I BLUSH WHEN YOU SAY
I HAVE A GHOSTWRITER

i want to believe you when you say i am not a 21-year-old girl but an old lady from Brooklyn, glowering from the corner of a crowded subway station as i blow smoke rings through the sticky, orange "O" of my lips. i want to be unapproachable, so when you come towards me i can pummel you with my trapezoid purse.

HOW TO BURN ASHES

Do you remember your first time there,
how you stood on tiptoe at that glass counter
where they kept the battles, your heart
trampling your chest at the thought of choosing
your own? How they placed one in your palm –
such ceremony, that constant smolder
you mistook for satori? There was a time
you'd sit up at night, kissing its rough edge
to your wrist, your nerves
screaming for mercy. Remember
how perfect that pain was, the usual ache
made holy simply by being yours for once,
being chosen? You knew it wasn't real strength,
those hot tingles – for all their acuity –
imbuing you nothing. But a sting
like that brands you for life. A sting
like that never lets you forget how fucking good
it used to hurt. After that, it doesn't matter
who your lover is or that when they pluck those
strings that stretch across your shoulder blades,
the song could make a god fall to his knees
and weep. Because you're no god. You're a box
of wet leaves that pleads to be burned,
this whole world a match. And you
keep striking. Don't you?

MYSTERY FLAVOR

I have this theory about mystery-flavored lollipops,
which is that we don't really know what we like or how they taste,
that if any of those flavors were sold on their own, in packaging
reflecting what it meant to hold them to our tongues, nobody
would bother. Like that time when, despite all the warnings,
you drove in the blizzard and your car spun out
in the middle of the freeway, how the words "fender bender"
became almost a blessing, those 400 dollars
a small price for absolution. Those days Erie thaws
just enough to yank itself from winter and people
tan on the still-wet benches like 40 is the new 87.
They aren't really warm in their board shorts,
and no crash is ever a blessing. You fight with your lover
and swear you feel the end coming and it's not
pleasure when she touches you next, just the relief
of knowing she is still there to be disappointed
and you to be redeemed. None of the mystery flavors
are any good, or if they are we'll never know.
It's just pessimism making us lucky, and desire
is less about what happens than our expectation
of loss. We mistake fear for gratitude,
living in the space between all the horrors
we could have unwrapped instead. The things I think of
now as you wait in an ER a hundred miles away
for a verdict I'll pick to pieces.

MEDITATION ON LONELINESS WHILE TEARFULLY BINGE-EATING HONEY NUT CHEERIOS IN MY UNDERWEAR AT 3:47 A.M.

you know that thing where, right before a big tsunami hits, the sea gets sucked away and over the curve of the earth?

THE EIGHTH DAY

On the eighth day Adam and Eve got restless
and began exploring each other's bodies.
First Adam took her soft face in his hands,
told her not to be ashamed and fuck
what her father said and then slid her open blouse
off of her shoulders and began to kiss her.
She accepted, breathing hard in all of the right ways
but he felt her shaking. He asked if this was her first time
and she said *kind of* and he said *yeah, me too,* her fingers
trailing his skin like you do when you've just moved into
a new place and you feel around for your subway stop,
your morning coffee and Rite Aid. She didn't yet know
where any of it was or what it did and spent a long time
comparing it to what she had, like an inventory of veins
and forms and creases. It was all the same except
for a few things and when she touched them he said
suddenly, I think I know what we're supposed to do.

throwing yourself on that serrated edge
will not love it into softness.

SAVED

I once fell for a guy who loved Jesus
and wanted me to love Him, too – not
like a fire-and-brimstone howler on the street
corner but a man trying to acquaint you
with his best friend. Like your best friend
trying to set you up on a blind date
with someone they work with. Like
he hoped one day to invite both of us
to the same bar and when Jesus looked up
from His water glass of Merlot, I would know
exactly who He was, no introduction needed,
just, "Hi, I've heard a lot about you," and
that would be that. Maybe I could order Him
a Three Wise Men and the three of us
would share a smile, in on the same joke.

He in turn fell for the Jesus-shaped space he saw
inside of me, not like a particular need
or a calling but a vague opening where,
if you jammed Him in hard enough, the Lord
might have fit. But the curiosity that he admired
was not an invitation. Not ignorance,
not a void aching to be filled. Only a love
letter to the unknown, a reverence
toward the many ways people like him tried
in vain to shed some weak and incomplete
light. Two wires had simply crossed
when they weren't supposed to and here
he was, pining for me to step out
and stop feeling around in the dark. He didn't
understand that I liked it in there, that my own awe
was the only thing I had any interest in believing.

One night, he said via instant message
that he felt Jesus lightly tapping at my soul,
and suddenly the Lord was no longer a friend
of a friend that I might like to meet someday
and more like an older man in a bar who
wouldn't leave me alone. Now
I picture Him purring in my ear that He can turn
water into wine, His one-off gimmick bar trick
that He thinks will let Him take me home.
I picture myself numbly sipping my vodka cran
and hoping He'll leave. I picture His friend hovering
behind Him with a kind of mechanical smile
and later asking me, "Doesn't it feel so good
to finally be saved?" Now when I shut
off my light and lie there in the black,
waiting for the drowsiness to hit, I can still remember
the unholy strain in his voice.

WATER IN THE EYES AND ALCOHOL IN THE EYES ARE PRETTY MUCH THE SAME I KNOW THIS FROM FIRST HAND EXPERIENCE

Either both of these are cleansing or neither is. Makes no difference what jug dangles above you while you kneel with your arms outstretched, cupping only the air. You are looking up from a dirty floor at a face you can't make out and waiting for it to hit you. You squint ahead of you and see a void. You check behind you and see another 40 days in the desert, and you are so fucking thirsty. You are a desperate vessel, a rickety glass trying for once to hold something it can see. You are okay to drown now, knowing how it will happen: quickly, your neck craning up toward a dusty, flickering light that will make you never want to look at anything else again. Either both of these are baptism or neither is.

Wet flesh is wet flesh.

So, the stream might miss my mouth more often than it doesn't. So, it might splash up into my eyes, gather with wet thuds on the floor. Let it. I will bathe in it until even the hardwood is reeking. I will light the match and go down the way all of us do eventually: burning, with no place left to pour.

SAY WHEN

Next time, I'll make you dinner. Pasta. I'll cook
everything, and you, flawless as you are, will serve
both of us but eat from the palms of my hands,
layer the penne, the sauce, your unassuming fingers
gripping the all-important parmesan cheese shaker.
Say *say when* and wait as your wrist goes sore
and starts to shake so you have to switch.
You'll eventually run out. You'll get up, drag
your keys off my nightstand, trudge through
cheese-dust to the front door, the yeasty aroma
wafting through the apartment enough to nauseate
us both, the expired red sauce near-fossilized
at the bottom of the serving bowl. And, as your car
hums through the window screen, I'll whisper *when*
under my breath, like I have a choice. Like,
had we gone shopping beforehand, my plan
would have been foolproof, and I would be
sitting beside you still, eyes glistening, reverent,
still receiving your cheese sacrament uninterrupted.

I'M AFRAID

it's 1:05 AM on a work night
and i'm afraid to write a poem.
i'm afraid of finding out
the version of me who worries
about it being 1:05 AM on a work night
is not very good at writing poems.

i'm worried that a poem isn't like a bicycle
but a family dog
and if you come home from a hard day at work
and forget to lock the gate,
it'll charge off
down the block
and never find its way back.

i have forgotten to lock the gate
every single day for a month
and i'm afraid to go into the backyard.

so i don't.

i shut the curtains and the weeds
snake up the side of the house,
strangle the gutters, strangle everything.

eating honey-roasted peanuts in bed
as the shoots overtake the windows,
i feel something a little like lightness
and close my eyes with weird acceptance
for the day the tendrils curl in fists
around the latches and none of them
will open.

ON CONFIDENCE

Why doesn't anyone say it? Why
must we pretend this forced detachment
is pride, something that fills the emptiness?

It's lonely to be yourself, to be
ugly and marked for desertion –
the bruised apple in a perfect display.

The rewarded tell you to be your own reward
but never look you in the eye, seduced
by their reflections in the shimmering prize.

It's hard to tell sometimes if they mean it to hurt
or if they actually believe it, lost themselves
in the illusion that acceptance is rightfully earned.

If only you were more confident, more positive,
or more like yourself, maybe they would love you,
but they don't know those things when they see them.

They get uncomfortable if the ugly look
at themselves and see ugliness. They flinch
in empathy at each flawed face that touches the light.

They can't bear to see your ugliness, your pain.
They want you to indulge their delusion,
to show them that what is Real always prevails.

Because they look into themselves and see nothing
real. They look into themselves and see a knot
they don't know how to untie.

They look into themselves and see that they, too, are lonely, and they can't bear it any more than you can.

THE POET CONFRONTS
BUKOWSKI'S GHOST

On the night that I open my first MFA rejection letter,
Charles Bukowski appears in the corner of my college apartment
in stained khakis and a yellowed white undershirt,
swirling Jim Beam in a lowball glass. "Baby," he says,
the whiskey-dipped ribbon of his voice swirling out
into the still room, "remember

that day in high school
when we first talked
through your Apple headphones?

You were only seventeen
and blowing off class
but even then you saw
something special
about me. You
walked home
in a fog, altered
like old dads are
in their stories
of listening to Pink Floyd
for the first time,
the world falling to me.

Isn't that right,
baby?"

It's been a long night of self-insult, so my eyes are
glassy when they let go of my lap and find the creases of
his face, and my cheeks are scarlet-soggy from all
the crying. He curls his thin lips into a smile, which opens,
his teeth flaring in all directions like the keys of an old piano,
like in the video where I heard him read "Bluebird"
for the first time. A knot inside me tightens the way
it always seems to when a man is about to refuse to let me
get away with something important. "You think I don't see

you in there,
behind all the shivering?" he
says. "You are still
that girl who wanted
to be like me. You can't
get away from that."

He's got me, so I don't move. Slowly, his airy presence
inches its way to the spot beside me on the floor
where I've been tearfully shaking, resting on my thigh
with the vapor of his fingers, colder than death.

"That's why
this is so hard
for you, baby.

That's why this moment
feels like a lie.

That's why
you write poems
about self-love
then scratch your wrists
to pieces
on the bathroom floor,

why you condemn men
who buy their girls flowers
but secretly wonder
why you aren't
pretty enough
to have ever received them,

why I'm still your favorite
years later,
even after I've beaten
women behind your computer screen
too many times to count,

why the man
who stole your poems
and told you
the only thing you could ever be
was a girlfriend
still appears in your dreams
and holds you down
hard
and tells you what to do

and why you sometimes
don't mind that."

His ghostly fingers trail upward. I say nothing, thinking
of those paranormal shows I used to watch
late into the night, how the specters would enact
their slow, parasitic violence. His whisper lands
like a thousand cigarettes being put out on my tender neck,
all blasé fake-cool and ash. "You like to hurt," he says. "You

like it
when I tell you
don't try.

Rejection
for girls like you
is just permission."

The knot in my stomach releases to pleasant heat. This does it
for me. I hum in satisfaction, gazing at the dirty old man
with half-lidded eyes. My hands find his crotch without thought,
as if by some animal instinct I'd forgotten. He trembles.
"You know," I coo, all sugar and smoke, "you were wrong
about me." Bukowski's ghost gulps, frozen with lust,
and that's when I go for it, a full year's anger boiling
and pulsing in my fingers. With agonizing force, I grip both
of Charles Bukowski's phantom testicles, numb
as his ghostly cry wobbles the walls of my shitty bedroom
in my shitty apartment. "I don't need permission," I say,

and I squeeze until all the pain is gone.

VOICE TO TEXT

I met Nathan on Yik Yak
when my Greyhound stalled in Edinboro
coming home for Thanksgiving.

When I found out he was blind, he asked
me to describe how I looked via text
in a way that he could understand.

I'll never forget the stress of trying
to sketch my own beauty, thinking to myself,
what decent poet would struggle with this?

The weight of that task: fumbling
to capture what he would never see,

the presumed expert on this thing
I didn't believe I had ever seen myself.

NARRATIVE

I've been thinking of narrative,
how sometimes the loose ends just fall off –
so little ceremony it's almost insulting.
People break up in movies and books
all the time but none of them have
given me the language for this sudden
acheless grief. I dig deep, scrape
some hard bottom where nothing bleeds.
You look up and your eyes are a plea for reason,
like a warm stone I can cough up
into your palm and my only sorrow
in this is there isn't any, that by the time
I went to tongue the sand into something real
you could trace, it had all been swallowed.

Not too long ago was that Christmas tree
you bought me, boxed-up in your Nissan Rogue.
I speed-walked down 4th, floating
with you behind me, rushed you and it
through the door with my fingers
straining to recall what it was like
out of the cold. There was a relief
in that elevator, the first breath in a while
not to crystallize a micron outside
our lips. Do you remember?
It was so warm inside.

ARS POETICA II

after a long night of crying,
you wake up with an entire durian in your throat
and retch it onto the empty half of your bed.
it won't open, no matter how much you squeeze, and your life
becomes a blur of cold ramen and calling in sick
to spend the whole day icing your purpled knuckles alone.

so when you feel that first warm trickle down your wrist,
it almost doesn't matter that what you're feeling is blood
or that it's your own or that the fruit is still closed
and mocking you from on top of your desk,
only that it makes those friends who have never seen fruit
stop sighing like that, confuse pride with relief.

before you know it, there's this boy begging
to lap what he thinks is wet sugar from your wrists
and you let him, pray to yourself it's not poison,
then pray to yourself he never finds out that it is.
you fall asleep on a still-empty stomach, Googling
how to bleach that red ring from around his mouth.

you blink, and now you're stowing vials in your bra
at parties, selling shots to people with durians
tattooed on their ribs. you watch them weep
and dance on each other, and then you slip out
before anyone gets sober. at home, you kick
a sack of durians from your front door and admire
how the TV's blue backlight makes your thin skin shine
like a Ziploc you can stare right through to your bones.

there is no empty side of your bed anymore,
just a torso of durians in various states of decay.
it makes you miss the boy enough to drive to his house
but find only the news that he died of some slow-bleeding
ulcer, left a goodbye note singing your praises.

that night you take off with nothing
but three dozen rotting durians on your back,
making one stop across town to pitch them into the bay.
it's *holy fuck* and *hell yeah* and your legs
hanging over the dock and pitch-black water.
you're going to change your name and move
someplace warm. you're going to dry up
and learn, like you should have, to swallow.

two months later, in Plano, your stomach engorged,
you wake up with this thing knocking
on the back end of your tongue
with nowhere left to go. you cough
and try to forget why it matters.

TO THE MAN WHO SAID READING MY POETRY WAS "MORE INTIMATE THAN SEX"

I think you wanted to shove your fingers
into those pieces I sent you, force them open,
drink what flowed out: *dark swirls*, or whatever
other phrasing you thought looked better
on your lips than it could have on mine.

It takes a certain kind of arrogance
to see the crystal surface of a lake at dawn
and dive in naked, the black silt clouding
as it loosens in waves from your folds.

You stiffen within them, ogling
small schools of tetra and tiger barb
as you interrupt their shape,
those roughly-fingered poems mere suggestions
you could rinse your feet in.

I should have known then that
whatever these hands made would be a hole.

YOU SAW YOURSELF IN ME
& WANTED TO DIE

this is the only thing people like us can be
to each other: burning
houses to go sprinting into, trying
to save something neither of us know how
to name. no need when we can close
our eyes, trace the same shapes
with our hands, bathe the same bloody dagger
in sunlight, convinced it's a flower.

what do we tell them?
it's like squinting into dark water and seeing
yourself in miniature. you think,
as if by instinct, *i hope it can breathe in there*,
and that's the first time you realize
you love it. it's like astral-projecting
above your own movie, silently
willing yourself to cut the right wire,
breathe air, drink water,
consider that throwing yourself
on that serrated edge will not love it
into softness.

it's you chain-smoking on my back porch,
saying you wish you were more
like the person i am with you.

it's me saying *me too*
and meaning it.

THE WORST MISSED CONNECTION
OF MY LIFE

I couldn't even unlock my own door
the day you came to visit, and I think
that should have been a sign.

But I wasn't thinking poems then, just
the sweat on my neck as I fumbled
with the old metal latches, blurting
I swear this is really my house,
I swear this is really my porch, hoping
all the while you'd laugh and stop smacking
that still-wrapped pack of
Camels against your palm. You were kidding

when you said *I don't believe you* but the world
had already shrunk to hand-size,
the lack of friction preceding it.

YOU LET A SNAKE LOOSE IN MY HOUSE

You let a snake loose in my house, forgetting
that every snake is actually dozens.

You let a snake loose in my house and balked
when one day I pulled seventeen from my purse
like a chain of colorful handkerchiefs.

You let a snake loose in my house without thinking
of the others who'd let their own snakes loose in my house,
of the way those snakes would love each other, their eggs
piling in the corners of my room, their spawn snaking
unseen behind the walls until nightfall when they'd squirm
out of hiding and collect in wriggling knots and knit
together, a trembling afghan of snakes, and hold me down
with their scaly bodies as they'd prick my flesh in my sleep.

You let a snake loose in my house and nearly went insane
when another one squeezed its way out of the showerhead
and slid down, limp and seizure-like, circling the drain. You were
so mad you turned the water off and left, dripping-wet
and barefoot, stomping through the carpet of snakes in
the hallway, to tell me that you'd found something disturbing
in my bathroom. That you'd been a gentleman and tossed it
outside for me. That this was my only warning, and you'd
leave me if I ever did something like that to you again.

NOTHING BUT OLD LINT

people keep telling me to be the bigger person but i want to be small. i want to squint and mumble curses 'til i end up someplace frustrating and dark, like your conscience or the toe of your sock. you'll throw up your hands on the street corner, kick off your boot and unveil your clammy sole to the masses. onlookers will wince as you wave the sweaty fabric in the air, trying to dislodge me. you'll scour the gold toe with your fat fingers and find nothing but old lint, and yet when you set off again, that slight pain will linger. it's a simple existence, but i'd do it for you: rot in my ill-wishes, become an aggravation so small it can't be seen.

YOU WILL BE SEEING UNUSUAL ACCOMPLISHMENT

Around the turn of the century, a man named Ed Leedskanlin fell in love with Agnes Scuffs, a sixteen-year-old girl, in their home country of Latvia. They soon got engaged, but on the day before they were to be married, she left him, citing their ten-year age difference as the prime reason. He then moved to the United States, where in 1920, he began building what is now known as the Coral Castle: a massive structure including two obelisks, a tower complete with furniture, and even a perfectly-balanced swinging gate entrance – all made entirely of limestone and constructed solely on his own.

Rare pieces of photographic evidence suggest that the five-foot-tall, hundred-pound man used practical methods, such as simple machines, to build the structures, but others assert that he must have harnessed secret (or perhaps even supernatural) energies in order to do so. Though Ed published many writings claiming that he discovered the secrets of the universe, he never divulged exactly how the Coral Castle was built, and his so-called "Sweet Sixteen" never saw what her scorned lover constructed in her honor.

It finally occurs to him,
as he leans on the wall of his finished monument
to love, that the girl ten years his junior never asked
for an obelisk, that those heavy stones he moved
had done nothing to move her, and she shouldn't
be blamed for the ache that settles now in his bones.

But he'll go on like being lovelorn is his only sin,
charging tourists ten cents to roam the tomb
of his heart, take pictures of the crude limestone slab
that he called "bed" and cut to the length of
her unfinished body. And they will call it beautiful:
his love alone enough to lift those hunks of earth
into meaning – some strange, ancient magic.

LETTER FOR A FAN

Fuck a book if I could just have another phone call
from you in an airport, the noise and the laughing lady
behind you, no cinema or pretense but this sole
sparkling highlight: my soul like a dead cell phone
finding momentary signal in trees at the edge
of myself. The white fog lifting over the mouth
of that dark hole, and you, shadowed, howling,
your fists clenched in catharsis. Now I know how
many times I thought I saw figures but didn't,
how many times a chorus was a desperate branch
snagging the wind, that none of the teeth I could pull
would make a necklace and why not. I thought the best
thing I'd hear would be something I'd ask for. I thought
the rhapsody was the one you played with a room
of men smiling at your back. But I know what makes
the virtuoso say fuck it to the orchestra: one guy
humming in a restroom stall alone, so taken by
the phrasing he doesn't stop even when someone
walks in, even when the flight is boarding, and
the lady behind him stops laughing to listen.

I JUST WANTED YOU TO KNOW THAT SOMEONE LOVES YOU BAD

With hands that go anywhere except your skin. A body that goes anywhere except your body. Not like the obvious: the wet warmth of places we pretend we've never been before, wearing each other's dewy skin like identical shirts a thousand kids buy to be different. Not a kiss I give you before leaving but an old coin you keep forever, rubbing in your pocket for good luck. Not because we don't want it, but because everybody does. Instead, I'll leave marks on you that the rest don't wear. A night that isn't an infinity-symbol tattoo. Be still. Let me hold you without holding you. We'll skip to my after-talk, these fractured nonsense moments before drifting that belong only to us. Tell me I can show you something you haven't seen in some video or mottled old portrait. I need to know there's something beyond all of our human trappings, beyond what we can dissolve in our mouths.

THE TRUEST POEM I WROTE ABOUT YOU

The truest poem I wrote about you goes
fuck you fuck you fuck you fuck you fuck you.

The truest poem I wrote about you is a sponge
that gets bigger every time you touch it
'til you're shriveled-up and gasping.

It follows you around, listing
your blunders and shortcomings
in a frequency only you can hear,
and then hugs you in public.

It proclaims itself the bouncer,
pretends there's a password, and asks you
to beg from your knees for it. As you walk in,
heaving, hair still tear-glued to your face,
everyone there gives it a hug and a high five
and thanks it for all it's done for this community.

Sometimes, it tells you nice things,
like you're pretty, like you remind it of a painting,
like you carry some jewel within you,
but it is only plagiarizing other poems
already written about other people.

Often, you say something funny under your breath
and my poem says it in a louder voice
and takes credit for the joke.

Every day, it moves everything in your apartment
one inch to the left. It doesn't know why
you keep bumping into all the furniture
but it thinks you two should go away for a while
and it can kiss your bruises while you sort this thing out.

The truest poem I wrote about you knows The Business.
The truest poem I wrote about you knows your needs
and has developed a product that will fill them, the shittiest
monopoly in fine print and lingo it knows you won't understand.

But the beautiful thing
about the truest poem I wrote
about you
is that you'll never get to see it.
Because this poem is best served as an empty threat,
a tease, the moment of eye contact we'll share
across the podium now that you know it exists.
Because you're afraid of this poem,
and you should be.

A POEM IS BULLSHIT AT THE BOTTOM OF THE OCEAN

as bullshit as a napkin, as nylon, those yellow coats
the kids marched in under clouds at the parade
i missed today, sleeping you off. though we drag
language with us at our ankles, there is still no line
for some frustrations, mysteries: the sameness
of every heartache just like you whom i've met
and will meet. how their metaphors
mix, strained and muddying. how i hurt
and you only craved me, seeing yourself
as a door, my life an unfurnished room, no
space. this ocean as thirst. how, cold
and sea-stuck, i'd weep for air within it
as your hands trembled water into a broken glass
and you whispered, "drink," spilling
onto and around me. today, it is sunny
where you are. a shaman guides you
to a lake, moves you to thirst.
in the distance, a flock of geese skim
the undrinkable water, their feathers
bending it to kiss the light. it's enough
to make you weep, and you might weep,
but it still won't be anything like satori.

I NEARLY HAD A PANIC ATTACK WHILE
RUSHING TO GET LUNCH BECAUSE
A MAN ON THE STREET WHO LOOKED
LIKE A GOBLIN STARTED SPEAKING
IN TONGUES AT ME & I'D HAD SO MUCH
COFFEE & HE WAS SO GOBLIN-LIKE
THAT I BRIEFLY CONSIDERED
THE POSSIBILITY THAT GOBLINS
WERE REAL & HE WAS A REAL GOBLIN

i feel like "The Reason" by Hoobastank
is the perfect song to play outside of your loved one's
window on a boombox after disappointing them
with your love for "The Reason" by Hoobastank.

WHY BEES STING (EVEN KNOWING WHAT WILL HAPPEN)

i'm not talking about the wave of rage
that comes when one is cut off
in traffic or buying groceries – that blip
of a primal urge to snap a neck,
disappearing too soon to be
rightfully acknowledged.
when she'd wound him,
disappearing at night to buy drugs
and re-emerge remorseless,
a hot-air gaslight full of bile
and fake babies, what i pictured
was not a cartoon death,
some kind of petty punchline. i wanted
to tear each shred of flesh from her small body,
wanted her skin in ribbons through the cracks
of my fingers. a novice, lacking the right
vocabulary for violence, I pictured myself
clenching some vague organ,
relishing fistfuls of something crimson and soft.
in the old tradition, wasting nothing,
i'd floss the meat from my teeth with sinew,
my neck a carabiner keyring of bitch bones,
knowing all the while the vicious unwinding
of entrails like streamers from a sad piñata
was still a holier sacrament than what she gave
him with her body – when it was still a body,
when i could still wonder
why bees sting, even knowing
what will happen.

i see all of the too-much, too.

FOLK SONG

They keep telling you to wait for a sign
and you find it at the mouth of a dark cave

at the bottom of the ocean. Everyone tells you
not to go down but you ignore them, suit up,

rehearse breathing. You know that no one has
ever come out of the cave alive but you

are no one in a different way. The cave is
talking to you, a language no one else can

hear, distorted underwater but earnest and deep and rough.
So you float down to the ocean floor. The mouth is

bigger up close, makes you tremble
as your feet touch down with a delicate pressure

on the murky bottom. *Sing me a song*,
the cave bellows. Your voice is a raindrop in a lake,

a roughed-up old coin in a shopping mall fountain,
the sound swallowed up by the vastness.

But the cave sings it back to you still, enchanting
with its wet eerie drone. You carry on,

song after song, these timid offerings. You kneel,
absorbing muddy echoes and wonder if this could be

what they mean when they talk about prayer.
You lie awake at night, picturing what lurks

beyond the entrance, become a wave
foaming through the cracks in the walls,

exploring their every etching. Needing
what you need, you stumble in,

your murmured lullaby warping and repeating
around you, echo-locating your way to

the back of the throat to find the man who lives inside.
You greet him and he grabs you, rakes his nails

into you roughly, terrified to be trembling
with another's breath. He kisses your forehead

and you see God. Pushing some hair behind your ear,
he says, *sing me a song*, and you sing together,

and the song is beautiful, unmangled, not yet
forced inside-out by some large swath of ocean

between you. When you stop to breathe,
you hear it, his tortured resonance, hoarse

and jaggedly beautiful like glass disfigured
from decades of tossing in the sea. You

tell him it's beautiful and the kiss he plants on you is
frantic. He claws at your skin and bites you,

pressing against you so your body nearly melts
from the pressure, becomes part of his own.

But just before it happens, he pulls away
from you, changed and meek now,

just some trembling shell. You ask him for
a sign, but he just stares past you

into the churning sea, eyes silent and dark. When you go
to kiss him goodbye, he grips your bicep, forces you

back out into the open water,
up the throat, out of the mouth.

You rise to the surface like a diseased fish
and tell everyone what you've seen.

Ready to prove it, you pull them down
with you, make them stare like you did

into the black mouth. And you sing again,
trying to recreate the time when you swore

his misunderstood beauty came surging out
through the indigo nothing. But it's just

your own voice bouncing back at you, warped,
maimed by the thick murk and the cold cave walls.

BEST BEFORE

Behind your door, we finger journals and maxi-pad boxes
for shreds of ourselves. In rare reflections, we catch
our oil-slick foreheads, boast our imagined glows,
counting each soft feather as it's lost in the wind.

Our ages betray us. Our mothers send us away
with old handbags, crumpled dollars. We discuss yesterday's
recess while feigning comfort ordering from the mini Starbucks
in the grocery near your house. We walk out
with the token macchiatos and cheap lipgloss but
also a can of creamed corn, proud
to have finally afforded an emblem for our long-term inside joke.

Someday, long since lost to sea, you will wash up
again, all legs and eyes, still clumsy from waking,
inform me our totem is still safe in your childhood
bedroom, years past the Best Before date. You will
offer to bury it with me the night of graduation but
neither of us will appear, except in a picture
our parents take of us by the bleachers, you
with your unwrinkled gown and dangling medals, me with
a piece of concession-stand chicken strip stuffed in my mouth.

LOVE DOESN'T EXIST, CHANGE MY VIEW

because i'm still writing about you.

because when i gave up on love-bites
i wore each bruise you left
as a badge instead.

because when the others couldn't see
the trick glimmer of candor in your smile
i stayed up during the storm
and held you.

because when you stepped on my heart,
i still fantasized about your hot breath
on its broken pieces.

because i never believe online pop-ups
that say "all dermatologists hate her!"
so when they said they hated you
i turned and scoffed
while i watered your grove of rotten apples
for her to taste.

because i moved across the state
and did it again –
unzipped my skin again,
let someone else suckle at my soul
without promising to stay again.

because despite your wicked
razorblade of a tongue
it's still a greater loss
to protect myself from others like you,
to refuse to water this dying garden
and miss the flower on the one day it blooms.

INTIMATE BIOGRAPHY OF A NARCISSIST

1.
He says he would kill to be this young, still undefined,
the ten years he has on me still spread on my apartment floor
like an empty map. He hurries to fill me with himself,
taunting, and I open for him, do what I always do
when I meet someone who gawks at me like a glass chandelier:
forget that a narcissist can only ever love himself, that I am
just a box of dirty mirrors.

2.
He wants me hanging above his bed like a row of paper dolls,
childish, wants to skim me like an à la carte menu,
folding back the parts he doesn't care for. My joy
bores him. My confidence disgusts him. My wholeness
disappoints him. He resents wanting me when I'm like this:
solid, no cracks for the light to pour in, no way for him
to gaze longingly at his own face.

3.
Still, we were friends the way damaged people are always
friends: ships refusing to budge as they pass in the night,
our hulls scraping each other, fetishists
for the way the paint flakes off before it hits the water,
never to be seen again. Another chapter in this lesson
I fail over and over, not ready to live without it.
Who are we if we don't leave these bruises on each other?
What would we have left to kiss when everyone walks away?

THE POMEGRANATE ONE

Every question I ask you is a pomegranate that splits open, spilling onto your carpet in dozens of tart little gems. Every time you pick one up to eat it, I stop you because I need you to enjoy the entire thing fully, which means not just eating the pomegranate but breaking open all of the little seeds, which are also pomegranates. Inside of those pomegranates are sometimes seeds and sometimes more pomegranates, but they look exactly the same and the only way to tell if you're about to eat a seed or a pomegranate is to try and put one in your mouth and gauge my reaction. But you can't just test them all to be safe, of course. Being wrong comes with the risk of being handed yet another pomegranate filled with – you guessed it – pomegranates.

So, we sit cross-legged on your floor while I watch you inspect each half-disassembled piece of fruit. It takes forever; nobody ever taught you to eat pomegranates this way. You're paralyzed with fear. And I'm wondering if you fear fucking up or just having to eat another pomegranate, which is in and of itself another pomegranate. And then I worry because you've been doing this so long it's starting to stain your skin and the floor. I wonder if you notice. That's a pomegranate. I wonder whether you'll get mad at me about the stains after you're done, and if not, whether you will later: two pomegranates. I wonder if getting mad would be right or wrong: pomegranate. I know you used to like pomegranates before but I keep thinking it's impossible for you to still be excited about them now. I keep this to myself. (You're welcome.)

By now they're starting to pile up in the corners of the room with no end in sight. You sigh and grip one in your shaking hands and you start to wonder if pomegranate seeds are even real or just a myth to get you to break open more pomegranates. But then you taste one, and everything makes sense for a minute. It's sweet, with that tinge of bitterness you remember, rich and light and so complex and satisfying, you wonder how it could possibly be good for you. Only one way to find out, so you open another. And now your living room looks like a produce section someone was murdered in, all red stains and bruised fruit. Now, they multiply before leaving my mouth as I wonder which are worth handing you and which are worth swallowing whole, and so on. I keep thinking that maybe there is something better I can do with these pomegranates, like make a jam or some kind of art project you can hang up and forget. But all I ever want to say is that I know I'm like this, and that I don't like pomegranates either, and that I don't mean to keep coughing them up into my hand. I want that to be enough. But it's another pomegranate to ask you if it is.

REAL WISDOM

for b.

somebody should have told me
you're just supposed to sort of throw a rug
on top of all of this
instead of trying to look at it closer.

that was my mistake.

just throw a rug on top of it
and build a really nice statement piece of furniture over it
and invite people over to admire your interior-design skills
and call it a fucking day.

it's true: if you see one cockroach,
there are definitely more behind the walls,
but you're never going to kill all of the cockroaches,
so you should just dispose of the ones you do find
and stop pulling up the floorboards.

but nobody ever tells you that.

IT'S FINE

for jason

despite what i may have said before,
i secretly like it: the men twice my age
in the state store trying to hide their smirks
as we stroll up to the counter, enough angst
for a crowd and one marked-down fifth
between us. moments clinking
beers in a dark bar when my eyes snag
on some guy whose stare reads,
"nice catch, dude!" a message clearly meant
for you on a frequency only i pick up,
your tuner pruned down to essentials:
small bills and sweat and dining in towns
so old they've forgotten their own names,
where the wolves of the new world lurk
and you pretend to ignore their sharpening
teeth. that's the intrigue. their reality
a stage where they watch only styrofoam
cutouts of what we are: freaks
endowed with a special kind of arrogance,
the burden of truth a grin we flash each other,
a joke no one is in on. that one
where we rip down the curtains
and something new happens, more holy
than touch. the dead language
for things the new one doesn't say:

*i love you
and the trash you're made of*

i see all of the too-much, too

*you're clearest to me on a road
that goes forever, mumbling poems
as you burn the endless tank, joints
in the glove box and* Astral Weeks
*in a thousand jewel cases
crashing together under the seats.*

POEM AFTER REALIZING YOUR ENTIRE FAMILY UNFRIENDED ME ON FACEBOOK

in an instant, i recall that they only love you
unconditionally, and a fist shuts inside me. it's not
that i'm changing my mind, that i should have kissed you
when you asked me from the middle of my kitchen
in tears last time we spoke. it's the deed love becomes
when it's time to sell the house, the fine print
of having nothing i own and how it doesn't matter
that none of the plants you've watered were yours
until you're not allowed back inside. i know
there are ways through this, but why are they all
surrender? there's a glitch in my empathy
and i don't know how to reverse our roles.
i think of your mom waiting in the car
the night she drove you to our breakup,
her arms at the end of my cruelty the real dividing
of possessions, and it occurs to me everything
i've ever held has been rented.

NO IT'S COOL, NEVERMIND, I WAS PROBABLY JUST BEING DRAMATIC

you know that thing where you're listening to The Flaming Lips in the late afternoon at your desk at work and you think about changing the song but then all of a sudden Wayne Coyne is saying how happiness makes you cry and the entire world feels slower and it's like suddenly you realize what they were all talking about — not The Flaming Lips, i mean everybody, every person sharing every sentiment you could almost touch and now all of a sudden you can, and it's like putting on a pair of glasses for the first time and you realize the trees have leaves on them?

CONSPIRACY THEORY

What if when they step out of the party, the first thing
they mention is your beauty, that cute crooked smile
the first bullet point in a recap of all the things they wanted
to tell you but didn't know how? Like the men left staring
after you in every subway car you've ever stepped off of,
who spend the rest of the afternoon wistful, wishing
they'd asked you what book you were reading. Maybe
you're the center of gravity in this bar and don't know it,
dragging whole worlds by the ends of your hair,
like a sun that watches orbit and sees only cold
rocks hurling themselves away and back. The boy
won't let you into his heart for the weather you make in it,
can't take the ache of those flowers blooming under your feet.
What if it isn't contempt that quiets them when you walk
into the room, but overwhelming awe? Who would bother
to write a poem about that? How would you ever learn the truth?

I LOVE YOU

I love you

that's it,
and i know
somewhere in the ceiling,
good old Chuck
sneers his scummy *don't try,*
swirls the remainder
of his goddamn whiskey
around the glass,
unimpressed,
smoking a cigarette.

but i love you too much
to love like the other poets
do: tar-colored,
hopelessly distant,

aiming guns
down their throats,

stirring bits of razorblade
into their kisses,

and fearing suffocation
too much to breathe.

POETRY IS NOT SELF-EXPRESSION

i mostly write poems because stripping naked and having you all stand in my bedroom and watch me scream at the ceiling seems like too much of a logistical nightmare.

PACKING THE WOUND

I invite you over one night because I need something new to pack the wound. It's unmistakably July outside and I have the window open, so when you pull up to the house, you can already smell it. You walk around back and catch a frame of me undressing it in the second-floor window, bathed in shitty flickering light. I pretend not to see you. You know what you're here for but still take your shoes off in the doorway like there's something left in the house to get dirty. I don't flinch when you appear beside me in the mirror, instinct leading your hands to the spot where I once believed I could hold something.

You pull everything out, so innocent. Each layer of stale gauze is soaked-through and rancid, reeking of egg rolls and flat beer, sweat and crusted-over coffee-mug bottoms. You peel them back, holding each one up to the ceiling like it'll catch. And then you reveal it: the gaping hole where it's all supposed to go, where everything goes eventually. For a moment you just squint into the blood-caked border of the thing, consumed by some kind of sick awe. You ask me, *what happened?* but all I can do is wince at the sting of unfiltered air on the bare flesh, my entire body screaming through its uncovered mouth. This is the worst part, the being exposed. *Get it over with*, I hiss, and I hand you the knife.

Slice by slice, you slough off the layers of yourself. I shut my eyes but still hear each piece slopping onto the floor, onto the other pieces. I can tell the cuts are clean. I'm impressed. I ask if you're in pain but all you do is gently move my hand away from the hole, layering each sheet of your flesh neatly on top of the last.
You plug the cracks with the stringy excess, wasting nothing. I only hear you struggle once, when you tear the gauze wrapping from the roll before winding it around my trembling body, using the extra on yourself. I open my eyes while you're putting your clothes back on, catch you struggling to unstick your sleeves from the still-raw skin.

We don't say anything, and you lie in the bed in your jeans while I hole up in the bathroom, perfuming away the rot. By the time I come back out, you're already asleep, your newly-roughened edges splayed out across both sides of the bed to avoid the pain of touching each other. I curl up in the space that's left, wishing there were a part of you I could hold without squeezing more of your blood onto the mattress. I wake up in a half-empty bed but while making my breakfast, I notice the tiny paring knife has already been washed and left drying in the rack.

TO YOU, AFTER YOU'VE READ MY POEMS

I've made you angry. You wanted me to
provide a service, and now that it's over
and I haven't shown you what you were
looking for, you feel ripped off, cheated, tricked.
But consider *The Persistence of Memory*,
how when the novelty fades, it can't help
but remind you of what your old friends used to draw
in basements with magic marker, heads
full of acid. Most artists can only see
what you saw then, can only feel that
stinging disenchantment you felt when
you realized, on seeing them in person,
that your idols are flat and crude imitations, tangible
extensions of emptiness failing to provide
the answer you were looking for. Most paintings are
small. Most painters don't know
a thing about being or oblivion.
You could say most are just fucking around.
Let me tell you now I never claimed to
know a thing about nothingness or how
you should live. My poems are cold wax sculptures
just real enough to entice you to touch them,
like the Mona Lisa is a pretty girl
you lust after until you learn she's not
over her high school bullies and her
shitty parents. Yes, it's tragic, but
isn't it also beautiful the way you ache
when she makes you remember? Isn't it
beautiful the way the crowds gather around her
still, desperate and awed
to be lost there together, squinting
at her tiny image through the glass?

Kat Giordano is a poet (1%) and millennial crybaby (99%) who lives in Pennsylvania. She's a co-editor of *Philosophical Idiot* and works for a law firm somehow. Right now, she's probably either apologizing to someone for apologizing too much or distractedly staring at a random point over that same person's shoulder while wondering if she should.

Look deep into my eyes. Take a deep, cleansing breath and clear your mind. You are getting very sleepy. Kat Giordano is cool. You like her.

katgiordano.com | @giordkat

www.ingramcontent.com/pod-product-compliance
Lightning Source LLC
LaVergne TN
LVHW041230080426
835508LV00011B/1139